Write On...

BIG CATS

CONTENTS

Meet the big cats!

Lions, tigers, leopards and jaguars are all big cats. The biggest is the Siberian tiger, which weighs about the same as three men! Big cats are powerful hunters. They have sharp claws and teeth.

Big cats are different to other cats – they are able to roar because of their voice box. A lion's roar can be heard 8 km away.

Spot the difference

The cheetah looks like a big cat and is about the same size as a leopard. However, cat experts put the cheetah in a group of its own. There are two reasons: firstly, it cannot roar; and secondly it can't pull in its claws like the big cats.

As well as the big cats and the cheetah, the cat family contains one other group: the little cats, which includes pet cats.

Not all jaguars and leopards are born spotted. Black ones are called panthers.

4

This is a panther.
Up close, you
can see its spots.

Write On...

The adjectives **powerful**,
fierce, **cunning**, **stealthy**
and **sleek** describe big cats.
Can you think of more adjectives
that describe big cats?

5

Big cat habitats

An animal's home environment is called its habitat. Big cats live in many different habitats, from deserts to rainforests and from marshes to mountains. These places provide food, shelter and room to roam.

The open grasslands of Africa, known as savannah, are home to lions and cheetahs. There is long grass to hide in and there are herds of grazing animals to hunt. Forests make excellent hunting grounds too, and cats are expert climbers. Tigers and jaguars live in steamy rainforests and swampy wetlands.

Easy-going

Leopards are the most adaptable big cats. They live across Africa and Asia in all sorts of different environments, including forests, mountains, grasslands and deserts. Snow leopards live in the harsh mountains of Central Asia.

Thick fur keeps the snow leopard warm in the mountains.

Despite their name, snow leopards are closer cousins to tigers than to leopards.

Write On...

When you write a story, the landscape can help set the mood. Try a tale on a remote mountain. Perhaps the mood is bleak and lonely – until your characters excitedly reach the top!

The Siberian tiger lives further north than any other big cat. It survives winter temperatures as low as $-45\ ^{\circ}C$.

Brrr...

Amazing bodies

Chasing, stalking, leaping, pouncing…
Big cats are agile movers! They are
skilful climbers and swimmers, too.
Every part of a cat's body helps
it to be the best possible hunter.

 Soft pads on the feet mean
the cat can move silently.

The sharp,
curved claws
are brilliant
weapons. They
give excellent
grip, too.

Write On...

Alliteration (repeating the
same sound at the start of
a word) makes your writing
more interesting. Examples
are **curved claws**, **massive
muscles** or **cosy coat**. What
others can you think of?

A cat's fur coat keeps it warm and also acts as camouflage.

 A cat's body is lean and muscular. The biggest muscles, in the shoulders, drive the front legs.

 The long tail helps the cat to keep its balance.

 A long, flexible spine allows the cat to move, stretch and twist. It lets the cat take huge strides when it runs.

The cheetah has powerful shoulder muscles and a long, bendy spine.

Cat senses

Catching live prey takes speedy reactions. Cats' super-sharp senses pick up clues about the world around them, then their big brains process this information. The tiger has the biggest brain.

Big cats use all their senses to pinpoint prey. Their ears funnel in sounds, while their nose sniffs in telltale scents. The sensitive whiskers have nerve endings that tell the cat where nearby objects are – very handy in the dark.

Eye spy

Although a cat's eyes point forwards, they are so large and round that they provide a wide field of vision. Cats' pupils, like those of many animals, adapt to the light. In the dark, they grow bigger to let in as much light as they can.

Cats eyes' have special reflectors to gather as much light at night as possible. That's why they shine in the dark.

A cat's sense of smell is almost 15 times stronger than a human's!

Cats' ears can point in different directions to pick up sounds.

Write On...

Connectives ('joining' words such as **when, after, but** or **because**) help you to write longer sentences. Try finishing off **The tiger stopped in its tracks when...**

Killer cats

Cats are expert hunters. Their lean, agile bodies are perfect for stalking and chasing prey. When it's time to go in for the kill, cats rely on their powerful jaws and razor-sharp claws.

Most cats hunt alone, but lions team up as a pack. All cats use the same basic hunting technique, though. First, they use sight, sound and smell to find their prey. Then they stalk it, creeping up silently and stealthily. Finally, they pounce or give chase.

Deadly bite

Cats may swipe at their prey with their heavy paws, but they make their kill with a single bite to the neck. Then, they gobble up their meal fast.

Cheetahs are the speediest cats – in fact, they are the fastest land animals. Their top speed is 120 kph.

Leopards have a sneaky trick – they haul their kill up into a tree to hide it from other meat-eaters.

Write On...

You don't have to be writing poetry to use words that rhyme. They give any writing a wonderful rhythm. Try **jaws** and **claws**, **eyes** and **surprise**, **kill** and **skill**.

A leopard closes in on a gazelle.

Pride in the job

Lions are the only big cats that work together to catch a meal. They are also the only cats that live in groups – other cats live alone. A group of lions is called a pride.

A pride usually has one or two adult lions, five or six lionesses and their cubs. When male cubs reach the age of two or three, they leave. They must either find a new pride to join or live their life alone.

Picking prey

The lionesses do most of the hunting for the pride. They sneak up on their prey. They often target a weaker animal that will be easy to pick off from the rest of the herd. They sprint towards it and bring it down.

Male lions are much more selfish than lionesses! They very rarely share their kills.

Lions hunt mostly when it's dark, but they spend about 20 hours of the day just lazing around!

Watchful lionesses observe their prey.

Write On...

Verbs are the 'doing' words in your sentences. Make them work hard. Instead of the lionesses going towards the buffalo, they could **sneak**, **prowl** or **stalk**.

Cat talk

Most big cats live alone, but they still need to communicate. They warn other cats to stay away or let them know when they want to mate. Cats use sound, scent and visual signs to get their message across.

 Big cats roar to tell others to keep off their territory. The lion has the loudest roar.

 Big cats leave scratch marks on tree bark and on the ground to show others that this is their patch.

 Both male and female big cats spray urine around the border of their territory.

 Big cat mums have scent glands between their toes. They leave behind smelly footprints that their cubs can track.

 Big cats threaten others using body language. They bare their teeth, crouch low, flick their tail and growl.

Write On...

An onomatopoeia (say *o-no-mat-oh-pee-a*) is a word that sounds like its meaning. Try out **roar**, **growl**, **purr**, **yelp** and **snarl**.

A tiger's angry growl says "Back off!".

Mother and cubs

Big cats are mammals, which means that they give birth to babies that look very like themselves. Newborn cubs are blind and helpless. They rely on their mum for food, shelter and protection.

Most cats, apart from lions, live alone. After a male and female come together to mate, they go their separate ways. A few months later, the female is ready to give birth. She finds a safe den, such as a thick bush or old burrow.

Caring for cubs

The big cat mum has two to four cubs, which she feeds on her rich milk. To make the milk, she needs to eat. She leaves the cubs to go hunting. Every so often, she moves her family to a new den, just to confuse any possible predators.

A lioness with her cubs

18

Cheetah mums have more cubs than other big cats – up to eight in a litter. That's a lot of hungry mouths to feed!

Write On...

Wow words are imaginative words that bring your writing to life. Brainstorm wow words about big cat babies, such as **daring**, **mischievous**, **scrawny**, **fuzzy** and **energetic**.

Lion cubs are born with spotted fur. The spots gradually fade as the cubs grow older.

19

Family life

A mother big cat raises her cubs for two years or more. During this time, she teaches them everything she knows about how to survive in the wild, including how to hunt.

Cubs drink only milk at first, but by six to eight weeks old they are eating meat brought back by their mum. From about 12 weeks, she brings home live prey, so the cubs can practise how to kill. Cubs learn from each other, too. Their play-fights and stalk-and-pounce games are great try-outs for real hunting.

Leaving home

Some time after the age of two, the youngsters are ready to leave the safety of life with mum. It's time for them to look after themselves.

Play-fighting cubs do not really hurt each other. They don't bite hard, and they keep their claws in – mostly!

Female lion cubs don't have to leave home when they're fully grown. They simply stay with the pride.

Write On...

Planning helps to organise your writing. If your story is about the life of a tiger cub, first jot down the key moments that happen at the beginning, middle and end.

Wrestling tiger cubs
try out the skills they'll
need for adult life.

Close cousins

There are about 35 species of little cat. They include the pet cat as well as wild cats such as ocelots and cougars. Like their big cat cousins, little cats survive in the wild thanks to sharp senses and fine hunting skills. They live in many different habitats all over the world.

Clouded leopards and ocelots are two kinds of little cat that have spotted fur. The spots, called rosettes, give the cats good camouflage in the dappled light of their forest homes. Cats with plain, sandy coats are more likely to live in deserts or grassy plains. They include caracals and cougars.

Domestic cats

The pet cat is the most famous little cat of all. Cats first began to live with people around 5,000 years ago. In return for guarding grain stores, they were guaranteed plump mice to eat.

The ancient Egyptians loved cats. They built statues of them and made mummies of their dead bodies. They even worshipped a cat goddess!

Write On...

An adverb is a word that describes an action. In **sneaked silently**, the adverb is **silently**. Can you think of more adverbs?

The serval's outsize ears help it locate rustling rats and other prey.

There are more than 70 breeds of pedigree cat. The strangest has to be the hairless Sphynx!

23

Big cats in danger

Today, there is less wild space for big cats than ever before. Much of their habitat has been cleared to make way for people's homes, farms and cities. Many big cats are in danger of dying out.

 Habitat loss is the biggest threat to big cats.

 People kill big cats for their beautiful coats.

 Some big cats are shot by angry farmers, after attacking livestock.

 Baby big cats are caught and sold as pets. Owners get a shock when their cute cub grows to full size.

 Big cats are sometimes taken from the wild to perform in circuses.

 In the last century, the number of tigers fell from 100,000 to 3,200.

 Amur leopards are one of the most endangered big cats. There are fewer than 60 left in the wild.

The jaguar is at risk because its rainforest home is being chopped down.

Write On...

Surprises, shocks or suspense keep people reading. If you're writing an article about big cats in danger, try to end each paragraph with an eye-opening statistic.

Saving big cats

Although big cats are endangered or threatened, the good news is that many organisations are working hard to save them. They can help stop big cat numbers falling and, eventually, perhaps even increase their populations.

One way to help big cats is to set aside areas of land as reserves or national parks. These places are protected and can never be cleared. Animals are safe here. Researchers often fit them with tracking devices so they can study the cats, understand them and help to protect them.

Essential work

Zoos and breeding centres help their visitors see how important it is to protect big cats. They also breed big cats for the future and look at ways to reintroduce them into the wild.

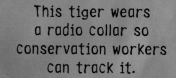

Wardens, guards and police all work hard to save big cats. They catch the people who break the law by killing or capturing big cats.

This tiger wears a radio collar so conservation workers can track it.

Write On...

Dialogue (speech) is a great way to hook the reader. You could start a story about a worker on a nature reserve with the words: **"STOP! Who goes there?!"** What happens next?

A few tourists still enjoy killing big cats as trophies, but most people agree this is cruel. The only acceptable way to capture a big cat is with a camera.

Write On... Writing school

Are you ready to show off some of the terrific big cat facts you've found out? First, decide on your form. Here are some ideas:

 A news story about a campaign to save jaguars – when you've finished, check if you've answered readers' possible questions about **where?**, **when?**, **what?**, **who?** and **how?**

 A poem or short story about a majestic lion – you could even present it on a lion-shaped piece of paper!

 A blog – write it from the point of view of a photographer who's looking for a panther

 If you like drawing, tell a short story in a comic strip, like the one below about tigers. How many frames will your comic strip have?

BEFORE THE TIGER GIVES BIRTH, SHE FINDS A DEN WHERE HER CUBS WILL BE HIDDEN FROM DANGER.

THE MOTHER LEAVES HER CUBS WHILE SHE GOES TO HUNT FOR SOME FOOD.

THE YOUNGSTERS SPEND A LOT OF THEIR TIME PLAYING. IT'S THEIR WAY OF PRACTISING HOW TO BE GOOD HUNTERS.

A diary is written in the first person.

This means you use **I** rather than **he** or **she**.

Add little illustrations to make it feel more personal.

11 AUGUST, HIMALAYAN MOUNTAINS

Today, I saw the mother snow leopard at the entrance to her den with the cubs. She'd just fed them but they weren't at all sleepy. They are six weeks old now so they still only have milk. In a couple of weeks, though, their mum will start bringing them meat to eat – blue sheep or ibex, a kind of wild goat.

The mum and her cubs

Glossary

adaptable Able to become used to new surroundings.

agile Able to move quickly and easily.

camouflage Colours or patterns that help an animal to blend in to its surroundings.

desert A dry place where little or no rain falls.

endangered In danger of extinction (dying out forever).

field of vision The entire area that an animal's eyes can see.

flexible Able to bend or stretch easily.

habitat The place where an animal or plant lives.

litter Young animals born to one mother all at the same time.

mate To come together to breed (produce offspring or babies).

muscular Having well-developed muscles.

national park An area of land that is protected by the government.

pedigree Pure-bred cat whose birth has been listed with an official cat club, and whose last three to five generations of ancestors are known.

pupil The black 'circle' at the centre of the eye, which is actually an opening that lets in light.

rainforest A thick tropical forest where heavy rain falls every day.

reserve An area of land kept for a special purpose, such as providing a safe place for animals.

savannah The open grasslands of Africa with no or few trees.

territory The area that an animal lives in and defends from other animals.

tracking device A radio collar, chip or other device that sends out radio signals, allowing the whereabouts of its wearer to be tracked.

urine Waste liquid that collects in the bladder and is passed out of the body.

Further reading and websites

READ MORE ABOUT BIG CATS:
Animal Attack: Killer Cats by Alex Woolf (Franklin Watts, 2013)

Animal Instincts: A Fierce Lion by Tom Jackson (Wayland, 2014)

Usborne Discovery: Big Cats by Jonathan Sheikh-Miller
(Usborne Publishing, 2008)

READ MORE ABOUT BEING A GREAT WRITER:
How to Write a Story by Simon Cheshire (Bloomsbury, 2014)

How to Write Your Best Story Ever! by Christopher Edge
(Oxford University Press, 2015)

The Usborne Write Your Own Story Book (Usborne Publishing, 2011)

DISCOVER MORE ABOUT BIG CATS ONLINE:
www.nationalgeographic.org/projects/big-cats-initiative/
Facts about big cats from National Geographic.

www.bbc.co.uk/programmes/b008pbyj
Clips from the BBC's award-winning series following the lives
of big cat families in the grasslands of Kenya.

www.bornfree.org.uk
Website for the Born Free Foundation, an organisation that campaigns
to protect endangered species in the wild, including big cats.

Index